Thank you for letting your light shine
for Jesus and planting seeds of
knowledge of Him in the tender
hearts of children
at Power Lab this week.
In His Love, *Lori*

Six Steps to Spiritual Revival

SIX STEPS

to

SPIRITUAL REVIVAL

LIFECHANGE BOOKS

PAT
ROBERTSON

Multnomah® Publishers *Sisters, Oregon*

SIX STEPS TO SPIRITUAL REVIVAL
published by Multnomah Publishers, Inc.

© 2002 by M. G. Robertson

International Standard Book Number: 1-59052-055-6

Cover image of stairs by Photonica/Toshiya Kumakura
Cover image of sky by Photonica/Naoki Mutai

Italics in Scripture quotations are the author's emphasis.

Unless otherwise indicated, Scripture quotations are from:
The Holy Bible, New King James Version © 1984 by Thomas Nelson, Inc.

Other Scripture quotations:
New American Standard Bible® (NASB) © 1960, 1977, 1995 by the Lockman Foundation. Used by permission.
The Holy Bible, New International Version (NIV) © 1973, 1984 by International Bible Society,
used by permission of Zondervan Publishing House
The Holy Bible, King James Version (KJV)
The Living Bible (TLB) © 1971. Used by permission of Tyndale House Publishers, Inc. All rights reserved.
Holy Bible, New Living Translation (NLT) © 1996. Used by permission of Tyndale House Publishers, Inc.
All rights reserved.
The New Testament in Modern English, Revised Edition (Phillips) © 1958, 1960, 1972 by J. B. Phillips
The Holy Bible, English Standard Version (ESV) © 2001 by Crossway Bibles, a division of
Good News Publishers. Used by permission. All rights reserved.

Multnomah is a trademark of Multnomah Publishers, Inc., and is registered in the U.S. Patent and
Trademark Office. The colophon is a trademark of Multnomah Publishers, Inc.

Printed in the United States of America

For information:
MULTNOMAH PUBLISHERS, INC.•POST OFFICE BOX 1720•SISTERS, OREGON 97759
Library of Congress Cataloging-in-Publication Data

Robertson, Pat.
    Six steps to spiritual revival : draw near to God and He will draw near to you : cleanse your
hands, you sinners, and purify your hearts, you double-minded (James 4:8) / by Pat Robertson.
        p. cm.
    Includes bibliographical references.
    ISBN 1-59052-055-6 (pbk.)
    1. Spiritual life--Christianity. 2. Religious awakening--Christianity.   I. Title.
BV4509.5.R625 2002
243--dc21   2002009202

02 03 04 05 06 07 08—10 9 8 7 6 5 4 3 2 1

CONTENTS

INTRODUCTION

NATIONS, AS WITH INDIVIDUALS, experience distinct spiritual cycles.

From seasons of strong spiritual fervor, nations throughout history have slipped into days of deep moral and spiritual decline—times when it seems that anything goes.

The Old Testament repeatedly chronicles eras when the nation of Israel (or her sister, Judah) turned away from God to worship heathen idols and adopted the wicked practices of surrounding nations. During those dark days, innocent lives were slaughtered; the rights of property owners went unprotected; corrupt, apathetic judges filled the courts; the poor were trampled underfoot by the rich; and the temple of the Lord fell into decline and disrepair.

As a result, the enemies of God's people were emboldened to invade, pillage, plunder, and enslave the towns and villages of the Promised Land.

But that which cycles down may also cycle up.

Those who have wandered away may return once again.

The pages of Scripture also chronicle those crossroads in Israel's history when the people turned back to God with all their hearts…times when God returned their former material prosperity and gave them safety and peace in the midst of hostile nations and uncertain times. As the Israelites cried out to God in broken repentance, they began to recapture the spiritual glory—and then the material and political glory—they had squandered away.

These unique and precious days in history—these rare-as-diamonds moments when individuals and nations return to God from apathy, apostasy, and idolatry—are called *revivals*. The term means "life again."

The bad news for us all is that without constant diligence, spiritual fervor will fade away. Practices once thought abhorrent become accepted. Little offenses that at one time were not tolerated begin to mature into murder, rape, kidnapping, and larceny.

The good news is that a loving God has said, "You will seek Me and find Me, when you search for Me with all your heart"(Jeremiah 29:13).

In the beginning of the twenty-first century, God is sending a message to the United States of America and to many nations around the world, urging them to turn from wickedness and spiritual apathy and to discover again His love, forgiveness, and protection.

What God speaks to nations, however, He speaks first to individuals. To you and me. The cry of each of our hearts should be "O LORD, revive Your work in the midst of the years!" (Habakkuk 3:2). *Start revival in my nation, O Lord, by first starting it in me.*

I pray that the simple truths expressed in this small book might cause you to experience a revival in your life such as you have never known before…and that the glory of almighty God and His Son, Jesus

Christ, might be revealed to you in all its awesome fullness.

Pat Robertson
Virginia Beach, Virginia

STEPS TO REVIVAL

*Draw near to God and He will draw near to you.
Cleanse your hands, you sinners;
and purify your hearts, you double-minded.*

JAMES 4:8, NASB

YOU KNOW HOW IT IS WITH CERTAIN TUNES.

Music has a way of unlocking memories. Sometimes all it takes is a little snatch of melody— someone humming as he walks by, a fragment of song from a car radio drifting through summer-night air—

and you find yourself reliving an emotion you thought you'd left behind years ago.

That's the way it is with me when I hear one particular hymn.

I was living in New York City forty-five years ago when I met Jesus Christ as my Savior. As a brand-new believer in 1957, I volunteered to be a counselor during the landmark Billy Graham Crusade that roused and stirred the great city for sixteen weeks in the summer and fall of that year.

What a kaleidoscope of memories surrounds that event in my life! I'll never forget it. The humid nights in Yankee Stadium…the massive crowds lined up outside Madison Square Garden…the traffic…the excitement…the singing…the television cameras…the fresh outpouring of God's Spirit. Those among the opening night throng will always remember the young black preacher, Martin Luther King Jr., who strode up to the podium and gave a ringing invocation. Two million people attended that crusade back in the Eisenhower era, and over fifty-five thousand gave their lives to Jesus Christ—more than one-third of those under the age of twenty-one.

One simple melody brings it all back to me.

No, it's not "Just As I Am." Nor is it George Beverly Shea pouring forth "How Great Thou Art," a hymn that had its first real launch in those very meetings. The huge, joyful choir that stood behind the platform sang a song I'd never heard before—though it had apparently been around for many years. The words and music wrapped themselves around my soul....

> *Turn your eyes upon Jesus,*
> *Look full in His wonderful face,*
> *And the things of earth will grow strangely dim,*
> *In the light of His glory and grace.*

Tens of thousands of people in New York City— and millions across America via television—did just that back in 1957. They turned their eyes upon Jesus, and they were never the same again. Maybe that's the reason why this simple song always makes me think of the word *revival.*

Beyond those memories, however, I really can't imagine a better definition of the term. Revival— whether personal or national—comes with turning our eyes upon Him. Beholding Him. Contemplating

His holiness, beauty, and might. Gazing by faith at His wonderful face. Allowing Jesus, with His glory and grace, to invade our human condition. And in the light of God's radiant presence, the allure of the world, with its pleasures and material possessions, begins to lose its grip on our lives. It truly does! Our hearts become satisfied by our heavenly Father's love and care. In fact, we can find our hearts overflowing with a real and joyful sense of the nearness of God and with profound wonder at His goodness and grace.

Before you feel the comfort of His presence, however, you must first become aware of how lost and hopeless you are apart from His help and salvation. In fact, that's the first thing that needs to happen when we "turn our eyes upon Jesus" and begin to earnestly seek Him.

DUST AND ASHES

Drawing near to God's brightness, we suddenly become aware of our condition. The sin in our lives, which we first accepted as normal, becomes distasteful—and then loathsome. And I speak from experience.

There came a time in my own life when I realized

the utter emptiness of what I was doing. My pursuit of money and status was leading me to nothing but despair. Neither my position with a large corporation nor the small company I founded with two friends brought anything close to lasting satisfaction. In fact, the deeper into worldliness I went, the emptier I felt. I would later learn the enduring truth of Augustine's words: "Thou hast created us for Thyself, and our hearts are restless until they find rest in Thee."

The restlessness Augustine described so well was building to a great intensity within me, and I finally came to the point of fully surrendering my heart, my life, my will, my total being to the claims of Jesus Christ. And there indeed—in Christ's salvation and in His purpose for my life—I found rest, a kind of rest far greater than I ever could have imagined.

Something happens when you catch a glimpse of Him.

The apostle Paul, who zealously pursued his own idea of righteousness before surrendering himself to the Lord Jesus, wrote that "if any man be in Christ, he is a new creature: old things are passed away; behold, all things are become new" (2 Corinthians 5:17, KJV). That radical transformation from old to new is exactly what happened to me when I received the Lord. It was as though I had walked through some sort of invisible curtain into a whole new world. I really didn't have to consciously think about ridding my life of sinful things. By God's grace, I simply had no desire for them anymore. I only wanted to know more of Jesus—His teachings, His love, His nearness, and His power. I had found the new wine of the Holy Spirit, which is far more satisfying than anything the world can offer us.

Such turning from sin happens to everyone who names Jesus as Lord and Savior. And note this: It is almost always accompanied by an awakened awareness of our sinfulness—and heartfelt grief over our ungodly thoughts, words, and deeds.

Consider Job, the man God Himself described as the most righteous man of his generation: "There is no one on earth like him; he is blameless and upright, a man who fears God and shuns evil" (Job 1:8, NIV). But when Job caught a glimpse of God, all thoughts of personal righteousness blew away like mist in the wind. He cried out:

> "I have heard of You by the hearing of the ear,
> But now my eye sees You.

Therefore I abhor myself,
And repent in dust and ashes." (Job 42:5–6)

When Job saw God, any sense of his own goodness or worthiness simply vaporized.

"Behold, I am vile;
What shall I answer You?
I lay my hand over my mouth." (40:4)

Something happens when you catch a glimpse of Him.

You can see the pattern again and again throughout the pages of the Bible. First comes an awareness of God, in all His power and glory. And this is immediately followed by the acute awareness of our sin and our unworthiness before Him. When Peter got his first taste of the power of Jesus the Nazarene, he fell at the Teacher's knees and cried out, "Depart from me, for I am a sinful man, O Lord!" (Luke 5:8).

In the first chapter of Ephesians, Paul composed a vast, sweeping anthem declaring the wisdom, majesty, and kindness of the living God. He follows this in chapter 2 with the blunt words: "And you were dead in your trespasses and sins" (v. 1, NASB).

Something happens when you catch a glimpse of Him.

I heard of a man who leaves his house very early in the morning for his job in the city. Thoughtful husband that he is, he tries not to waken his wife as he dresses and readies himself for the day. Knowing his closet by feel, he selects his clothing with care in the semidarkness of the bedroom and slips out of the house like a silent wraith. But sometimes as he steps off the city bus and walks toward his office in the bright morning sunlight, he suddenly begins to notice things he hadn't seen before. He observes the wrinkles in his slacks, the lint on his blazer, and the ugly stain on his tie.

What seemed perfectly acceptable in the dim light of his bedroom becomes totally unacceptable in the bright sunlight.

The prophet Isaiah had a similar experience. At a critical moment in Israel's history, after the death of a great king and leader, Isaiah had an overwhelming vision. One day as he was going about his usual routine, the heavens suddenly rolled back, and he found himself staring—in terror and wonder—at the throne of almighty God.

Almost at a loss for words (who wouldn't be?), the prophet did his best to record what he saw and experienced:

> In the year that King Uzziah died, I saw the Lord sitting on a throne, high and lifted up, and the train of His robe filled the temple. Above it stood seraphim; each one had six wings: with two he covered his face, with two he covered his feet, and with two he flew. And one cried to another and said:
>
> "Holy, holy, holy is the LORD of hosts;
> The whole earth is full of His glory!"
>
> And the posts of the door were shaken by the voice of him who cried out, and the house was filled with smoke. (Isaiah 6:1–4)

Something happens when you catch a glimpse of Him.

Now Isaiah was known in Israel as a great prophet of the Lord. He must have had a reputation as a gentleman, a solid citizen, and a man of God. He probably got out of bed that morning feeling just fine about his standing with the Lord. But what seemed acceptable in the dim light of earth suddenly became unacceptable in the fiery radiance of heaven. In that mighty river of pure light that flowed from God's throne, Isaiah looked at himself and was utterly appalled.

But what he saw was infinitely worse than wrinkled or blemished clothing. He saw the ugly stains on his own soul. How could such a soiled, shameful creature of dust like himself survive for more than a heartbeat in the presence of such awesome purity? The prophet cried out in his despair, believing death to be near.

> "Woe is me, for I am undone!
> Because I am a man of unclean lips,
> And I dwell in the midst of a people of
> unclean lips;
> For my eyes have seen the King,
> The LORD of hosts." (v. 5)

In Hebrew, you would have heard the piercing cry, *"Oohh-eeee!"* "Woe!" Just that quickly, he saw himself as "undone." Other translations use the words *lost, beaten,* or *ruined.*

Something happens when you catch a glimpse of God,

in His power and majesty and blazing holiness.

Isaiah must have fallen on his face, realizing his true condition before the Lord. But—God be praised!—the throne of holiness and might is also a throne of grace. He was forgiven and cleansed from his sin…and then God sent him out as a herald and spokesman to the people of his nation.

In revival, God first refines and purifies His people. Then He fills them with His power. He places in their heart His love and compassion for those who are lost—*beaten, undone, ruined*—without God and without hope in the world.

In revival, Christians aren't trying to work up the courage to testify about a historical figure they learned about from a book. Instead, they *radiate*—they can't help but radiate—the presence of the One whose power continually fills their lives (see Psalm 34:5).

Revival normally begins among God's people, but before long, like water surging through a broken levee, revival overflows and spills out into society. The power of God is so strong that prostitutes, drug addicts, alcoholics, and those addicted to gambling, pornography, and lust are set free and gloriously converted. In past revivals…

- saloons, dance halls, and theaters have emptied for lack of customers,
- jails have emptied for lack of criminals,
- courts have emptied for lack of disputes.

Can you imagine? Men and women found themselves drawn to spontaneous prayer meetings like iron filings to a magnet. Dealing with eternity became the uppermost concern in people's lives.

In the book of Acts, we read that the building where the believers gathered was shaken, and they spoke forth the word of God with boldness and joy (see 4:31).

TRANSFORMING FIRE

In revivals that have taken place in the Belgian Congo and also in China, young children have had visions of heaven. Some saw the second coming of Christ. Others, who had never been taught these things, saw the rapture of the church at the end times and believers being swept up into heaven.

In both the Congo in the twentieth century and during the frontier revival in the United States at the beginning of the nineteenth century, sinners entering prayer meetings fell to the ground where they lay for hours as the Holy Spirit brought their lives into conformity with His will.

In Indonesia, where believers were praying and worshiping God, it appeared to their enemies that the entire church building was engulfed in flames.

In China during the Boxer Rebellion, missionaries—aware of an angry mob rushing toward their building to kill them—huddled together to pray for God's intervention. Later, when they inquired why the mob had suddenly slunk away in fear, they were told, "Your building was surrounded by flaming warriors with raised swords."

Yes, in true revivals angels come calling, young men see visions, and old men dream dreams. God equips His people with gifts of the Holy Spirit, and they witness boldly about the wonderful works of the Lord.

During the past century in the United States, the term *revival* has normally meant a church-sponsored evangelistic meeting. Something programmed. Something planned months ahead of time, as a visiting pastor or itinerant evangelist comes to town for a week or two of special services. Churches put ads in the newspaper and notices up on their reader boards. Those who attend are asked either to make a first-time decision for Christ or to rededicate their lives to Him.

Can God work in such a setting?

Of course He can. And He often does.

But remember that He is ever more inclined to draw near to us than we are to seek Him. Although such evangelistic meetings can indeed bring about a true revival, their measure is usually limited to the number of people (few or many) who respond to the evangelist's appeals.

The revival that America cries out for today, however, does not consist of emotional preaching or even inspired evangelism. The revival we pray for transforms lives, empowers pastors, electrifies churches, rolls back the spreading blight of sin and national decay, and brings the *reality* of God to the entire population.

But how does such a thing come about?

How does it begin?

What are the steps to revival?

Over nine hundred years before Christ came to earth, God gave a simple formula to Solomon, king of

Israel, just after the dedication of the newly con-
structed temple in Jerusalem. Following a day when
the brightness and power of God's presence had so
filled the new temple that even the priests couldn't get
near the door, the Lord came to the king by night and
spoke to him. Even though that mighty nation's worship center was clean and fresh and new, God spoke to
Solomon about darker times—times when His people
wouldn't be so keen about sacrifice and praise and
obedience. What should Israel do when she had wandered far away from her God and stumbled into sin,
degrading practices, and hardness of heart? Where
should she turn when she began to experience the
righteous judgment of God for her unfaithfulness?

God gave Solomon the answer to that question in
advance. And I believe that as our eternal God looked
down the years, He also saw it as an answer for twenty-
first-century believers like you and me....

> "If My people who are called by My name will
> humble themselves, and pray and seek My
> face, and turn from their wicked ways, then I
> will hear from heaven, and will forgive their
> sin and heal their land." (2 Chronicles 7:14)

Who could put a price on a fresh, renewed walk with the living God?

Who could estimate the value to your neighborhood, your city, or even your nation if thousands and tens of thousands awoke to their deep need for Jesus Christ and His salvation?

It begins with you, now; holding this little book and simply *seeking Him* like you never have before.

Step One

HUMBLE YOURSELF

*Humble yourselves under the mighty hand of God,
that He may exalt you in due time.*

1 PETER 5:6

THE FIRST RECORDED SIN was neither lust nor larceny,
neither murder nor mayhem.

It was pride.

At some nameless moment in eternity past, an
angel of indescribable beauty and incomprehensible
power paused…to admire himself. And in that

26

moment a shudder must have run through the fabric of time and eternity. The destinies of countless angels and human beings changed in the twinkling of an eye.

The angel's name was Lucifer, star of the morning, son of the dawn. Since the day of his creation, he had declared the might and majesty of his Creator God. And then—though the Bible doesn't say how or why—something changed in his heart. Turning his eyes (perhaps ever so subtly, ever so slightly) from the Glorious One, he began to imagine glory of his own. Mistaking the reflection of God's radiance for some radiance shining from himself, he began to swell with pride and self-importance. The book of Isaiah records his very thoughts for us, as he declared:

> "I will ascend into heaven,
> I will exalt my throne above the stars of God…
> I will ascend above the heights of the clouds,
> I will be like the Most High." (14:13–14)

In that moment of pride, Lucifer became Satan. A creature of horror, dread, and the adversary of heaven and humanity until the end of time.

Humility, however, is the reverse of pride. And if revival begins at all, it must begin *there*.

MY WAY OR THE HIGHWAY?

The focus of pride is what *I* will do. My way, my will, my plan, my preferences, my sensibilities, my convenience, my understanding of the issues, my concept of God, my idea of righteousness. Just like Lucifer at the beginning, we want to exalt our throne, our way, our opinion, our methods, our ideas, our very person.

Without intending to, we begin to exalt those plans of ours above our allegiance to the Lord. We soon begin to neglect to take God or His will into account.

James underscores this attitude in his letter:

Just a moment, now, you who say, "We are going to such-and-such a city today or tomorrow. We shall stay there a year doing business and make a profit"! How do you know what will happen tomorrow? What, after all, is your life? It is like a puff or smoke visible for a little while then dissolving into thin air.... As it is, you take a certain pride in planning with such confidence. That sort of pride is all wrong. (4:13–14, 16, Phillips)

Do you see how subtle it can be? *"I'm going here; I'm going there. I'm going to do this, build that, buy whatever I like, and say thus-and-so."* We act sometimes as though we are little gods, in charge of our lives, in control of our destinies. But the truth is that every beat of our hearts, every breath we draw into our lungs, happens by God's permission and in His strength. Our very lives belong to Him, not to ourselves, and at any time of the day or night we might be only seconds away from standing in His holy presence.

Sometimes that truth slips from our minds. Despite knowing in our heads that our lives belong to God, we all too easily fall into the delusion that our lives are our own—to schedule and plan, to choreograph and design.

Do we pause to seek our heavenly Father's will before we make commitments?

Do we seek His guidance before we take on a project?

Do we pursue His counsel about our short-range plans—as well as long-range dreams and goals?

When we don't, when we find ourselves in need of a spiritual adjustment at the hands of the Lord, the results may be very painful.

In 1997, I was the chairman and controlling shareholder of a successful media company, which sold for a very large sum. I placed the bulk of my share of the proceeds into a charitable trust that would be paid to the Christian Broadcasting Network in the year 2010. My plan was to grow this money so that, when I retired, CBN would have adequate resources to fulfill its ministry.

A close adviser, however, suggested a particular investment that could potentially help me make significant progress toward this goal in less time. This supposedly "good deal"—one for which I was misled by that adviser and my insticts—became an absolute nightmare.

Before long, I found myself facing enormous ongoing expenses, time-consuming dead ends, and unexpected liabilities from the previous owners. For three years, I was in a trap that sapped my financial resources, my spiritual resources, and yes, even my joy.

Empty and exhausted, I rented a beach house at

the North Carolina shore for one week in August 2001 so that I could rest and pray. During that week, I cried out to the Lord for help, and He answered my prayer in a way that far exceeded my expectations.

First, God not only helped me understand the motives of my financial adviser, but He also gave me clear directions about what to do to get out of the trap.

Then, unexpectedly, God directed me to His purpose for America.

He assured me that a great spiritual revival was coming to America and that I should use the resources of CBN to strengthen churches and uphold pastors. He also gave me a plan for praying for that revival: We would call our audience to join together for fifty days of prayer for revival, and we would enlist at least ten thousand churches to join in that prayer vigil.

My life was changed. When I cried out to the Lord and asked Him to show me His design for my life and my ministry, He did just that. He lifted my self-imposed burden, and He gave me clear direction about what to do next.

We enlisted ninety-six thousand people to pray for revival for fifty days. Thousands of churches and prayer fellowships were involved, and I wrote the booklet "Steps to Revival" (the foundation for this book) in support of this nationwide prayer effort.

In God's sometimes strange providence, I began to see the answer to those prayers in the aftermath of the 9/11 tragedy that year. The Sunday after the suicide bombers hit the World Trade Center and the Pentagon, churches were overflowing. The nation was praying.

I was seeing God move.

Revival had begun.

We Americans were indeed humbled by the horrific events of September 11, 2001. Those not-to-be-forgotten television images forced many of us to our knees, seeking God's face. And that is the prerequisite for God hearing us, forgiving us, and healing our land. But just how long will those images prompt us to our knees? None of us like to be humbled any more than we like to be called "sinners."

CROSSCURRENTS

Is it any wonder, then, that at times we might find our pride—national as well as personal—running cross-current to clear statements in God's Word? God, for instance, declares a certain action or behavior to be sin, but we disagree. We question the "interpretation" of that biblical imperative or command, seeking to justify ourselves. We point to our friends who do the same thing and consistently get away with it. We argue that "everyone else" in society seems to accept this conduct. How could God reasonably question something so common and customary, so much a part of our culture?

Several decades ago, a line in a popular song declared that if something *feels* so right, surely it can't be wrong. That's the idea, isn't it? How could something that we enjoy so much possibly be wrong?

- If she's unhappy with her spouse, *what's wrong* with breaking up her marriage so she can be happy with me?
- Some doctors say marijuana might be medicinal, so *what's wrong* with a few puffs to take the edge off my tension?
- My boss doesn't pay me what I am worth, so *what's wrong* with "balancing the account" with a few supplies from the office?

- My neighbor tried to hurt my dog, so *what's wrong* with putting a few dents in his car in return?

Bit by bit, we begin to elevate our own sense of justice, our own formulation of right and wrong, over the clear teachings of the Bible.

Then there is pride of family, pride of physical appearance, pride of affluence and accomplishment, pride of material possessions, pride of nationality, pride of employment and position, pride of religious affiliation, pride of knowledge and education.

If we want to see revival—first in our own hearts and then in our nation—we must come face-to-face with the fact that we are creatures of dust. That before God we are all alike—weak sinners—and that there is *nothing* we possess that has not been given to us by the generous hand of God.

We must realize that our pride before Him is like the pus-filled sores on a leper. We must ask God to forgive us for the pride in our lives, whatever form it takes.

Jesus told the story of two men who went to the temple to pray. Both of them were Hebrews, both believed in God, and both entered the temple at the same time, but outside of those traits, they had nothing whatsoever in common. Luke tells us that Jesus "spoke this parable to some who trusted in themselves that they were righteous, and despised others."

> "Two men went up to the temple to pray, one a Pharisee and the other a tax collector. The Pharisee stood and prayed thus with himself, 'God, I thank You that I am not like other men—extortioners, unjust, adulterers, or even as this tax collector. I fast twice a week; I give tithes of all that I possess.' And the tax collector, standing afar off, would not so much as raise his eyes to heaven, but beat his breast, saying, 'God be merciful to me a sinner!' I tell you, this man went down to his house justified rather than the other; for everyone who exalts himself will be humbled, and he who humbles himself will be exalted." (Luke 18:10–14)

The despised tax collector went home that night savoring a refreshed and restored relationship with the living God. The bragging, prideful Pharisee did not—and, sadly, he may not have even recognized his loss.

Revival prayer starts when we humble ourselves, throw ourselves on the mercy of God, and plead for His forgiveness. It often begins with a single individual. From that small beginning, it ripples throughout a Bible study group, a church body. Soon, whole communities—even cities—fall at His feet, broken.

Humbling ourselves, however, means that we should never resist God or insist that our concept of right and wrong somehow supersedes His.

In the New Testament, we read that John the Baptist, speaking in God's name, called the people to repent and be baptized as a cleansing from sin. The Bible gives this amazing assessment of what the people did in response:

> And when all the people heard Him, even the tax collectors *justified God,* having been baptized with the baptism of John. But the Pharisees and lawyers rejected the will of God for themselves, not having been baptized by him. (Luke 7:29–30)

They *"justified God."* We can either justify God—in other words, acknowledge His assessment of our lives and actions—or justify ourselves. One attitude leads to revival; the other to spiritual deadness and inevitable judgment.

In which direction are we leaning?

Since September 11, I have been concerned that our country saw the tragedy as an opportunity for national reconciliation rather than repentance before God. When I suggested on television that God Almighty had lifted His hand of protection from America because of our sin, I was condemned on all sides. In fact, a poll taken some months later indicated that only about 5 percent of the American people acknowledged that the attack might have had anything to do with judgment for our nation's sins.

We've all seen the slogans and the signs, the flags and the bumper stickers. The messages on countless reader boards from Maine to California read "United We Stand," and "God Bless America." *But which America are we asking God to bless?* The America of our founding fathers…or the America we have become in the twenty-first century? Do we suppose that He will bless us just as we are—with our same-sex marriages, high abortion rate, blatant immorality in the media, abandonment of the traditional family, and mindless pursuit of riches and pleasure?

Even if a call for repentance had rung across the land on September 12 or sometime thereafter, would we have heard it? I doubt it. We tend to be too noisy defending our lifestyles, regardless of what the Word of God says about our activities and our choices.

"But I can't help it; I was born that way."

"Things would be different if my childhood had not been so difficult."

"I'm not hurting anyone else."

"He just doesn't satisfy me anymore."

"Everyone's doing it!"

Comments like these reveal our attempts to function as if we were king of the universe.

In so very many ways, Americans are not justifying God: We are neither accepting His holy ways nor bowing to His rightful rule of our lives. The fact remains, however, that acknowledgment of the sovereign Lord is the only kind of acknowledgment that leads to genuine revival.

We would do well to see less of the slogan "God Bless America" and more of the less popular phrase "America, Bless God!" This call to submit to God's lordship, to Christlike humility, leads to life. As we acknowledge God's justice and live it out, the Author and Giver of life will bless us, and I believe that His blessing includes His gift of revival.

Step Two

PRAY

*The earnest prayer of a righteous person
has great power and wonderful results.*

JAMES 5:16, NLT

THERE IS PRAYER, AND THERE IS **PRAYER**.

Most of us have found ourselves in a polite, well-dressed circle of people sitting in comfortable chairs in a pleasant room, legs crossed, praying nice-sounding words to the Lord. A fire crackles and pops in the background. Soft music, turned down low, whispers from the stereo. A plate of brownies waits in the kitchen, and the aroma of fresh coffee drifts through the room.

It's all very soothing and relaxing. But I have serious doubts that that was the kind of prayer going on in the book of Acts when the church gathered to pray for Peter.

> So Peter was kept in the prison, but prayer for him was being made fervently by the church to God. (12:5, NASB)

These were desperate days for the young church, and their prayers were desperate prayers. Stephen, a deacon, had been stoned to death by a furious mob. Persecution against the church of Jesus Christ had broken like a tidal wave over Jerusalem, Judea, and Samaria. The Christian-hater Saul and his storm troopers had only recently been going house to house, kicking in doors in the middle of the night, and hauling away in chains both men and women—fathers and mothers—to imprisonment and death.

King Herod had arrested Peter and James the brother of John. To the delight of the church's enemies, he had James run through with a sword. Peter waited in a dungeon, in chains, for his own appointment with the executioner.

It was a terrible time to be a Christian. It was a wonderful time to be a Christian.

Peter's execution would most likely take place at dawn—now only hours away as the church gathered to pray. This was no time for a quiet, genteel, armchair prayer meeting with cookies, chorus singing, and coffee. Acts 12:5 tells us that prayer was made "stretchoutedly" (literal Greek) by the church for Peter. It was constant. It was fervent. It was focused. It was all-out. I can imagine these dear saints weeping, falling on their faces, and crying out to God for mercy until their voices were hoarse. They did not pray aimlessly, nor were they distracted by stock market quotes or football scores or the latest government scandals or news bulletins. Their hearts had already been torn by the violent murder of James, and now Peter was in prison. *Peter!* The life of their beloved friend and apostle hung in the balance.

So the people of Christ prayed with every fiber of their being for Peter's release.

Most of us have never entered into *that* level of prayer.

Yet this is precisely where the power lies.

I'm reminded of a time over forty years ago when I prayed "stretch-outedly" to the Lord—and saw Him exercise His awesome power in a specific and unmistakable way. Life's circumstances definitely had me stretched out, praying with focus and fervency.

October 1, 1961, was approaching quickly, and that was the day when the new Christian Broadcasting Network, which I had been working for two years to start, was scheduled to go on the air with our first television station, WYAH-TV.

But only if we could come up with $7,500.

The owner of the studio equipment, the RCA Corporation, said that unless this bill was paid, we were not to turn on the equipment.

I had no source of money other than the Lord Himself, so I turned to Him. I prayed with an intensity and earnestness that was (I'm sorry to say) not normal for me. The future of the network was at stake, and I needed a miracle. Before I went to church that last Sunday morning in September, I opened my Bible to the Psalms. There I read, "The salvation of the Lord is at hand."

I believe, Lord, I prayed. *Your salvation is at hand!*

On the way to church I ran into a friend. In faith, I invited him to accompany me to the TV station for our opening broadcast. He accepted my invitation, and it was there at the studio that I explained my problem to him: No broadcast would happen unless I had $7,500. He put his head in his hands and then said, "I'll let you have the money."

That happened fifteen minutes before our scheduled airtime. This was indeed God's extraordinary answer to prayer—to stretched-out prayer!

I know of a quadriplegic woman who, because of her condition, has to be put into bed every night around seven o'clock. From there she offers her stretched-out prayers. Starting at about seven o'clock and going on until eleven or twelve, she prays around the world. Her prayers cover individuals, missionaries, pastors, ministries—even nations and world leaders. In those three or four hours every night, she enters into warfare, taking on forces of evil around the world, interceding, and pleading her case before the throne of God. No one outside a small circle of friends really knows about her ministry, but who can begin to calculate the power released from that little bedroom on that quiet residential street? Only eternity will reveal the effect of those faithful, stretched-out prayers.

James, the half brother of Jesus, tells us that "the effective, fervent prayer of a righteous man avails much" (James 5:16). As an example, he goes on to describe the prayers of the prophet Elijah, who *prayed earnestly* that it would not rain; and it did not rain on the land for three years and six months. And he prayed again, and the heaven gave rain, and the earth produced its fruit" (vv. 17–18). Literally this reads, "he prayed with prayer."

And God heard and answered.

A CRY IN THE NIGHT

Jesus told us to "pray always," and He gave us examples of what has been called desperate, or importunate, prayer. Allow me to paraphrase His story in Luke 11 just a bit.

Picture this scene: It's late at night. Stars fill the sky, and the neighborhood has been quiet for hours. You're deep in sleep, perhaps dreaming of floating along on the gentle current of a stream in your little fishing boat. Just drifting, drifting...and, *Wham! Wham! Wham!*

What in the world was that? *Wham! Thump! Wham!* You struggle out of the depths of sleep—half frightened, half angry, and thoroughly disoriented. "Open up!" you hear someone yelling. "Come to the door! I know you're in there!"

Alarmed dogs throughout the neighborhood begin barking in the night. Light from a few oil lamps appears in nearby windows. Who could be shouting at your door at such an hour? Who could be creating such a ruckus? Was there a fire? Were there robbers?

"Come on! Wake up and open the door!"

Suddenly you recognize the voice of your neighbor from down the street. What in the world could he be after in the dead of night? You open your second-story window and stick your head out into the cool night air.

"What?" you say. "What is it? What's going on?"

"I need to borrow some bread," comes the reply.

"You *what?*"

"I need a couple loaves of bread. I have a friend who just arrived from out of town, hungry as a bear, and the ol' cupboard is empty. I don't have a thing to put in front of him!"

"I can't believe this! You woke me up in the middle

of the night to borrow *bread?* You're crazy. Go home. I'm going back to bed."

You quiet your whimpering children, mumble an explanation to your wife, and crawl back under the covers. Slowly the tension eases out of your shoulders. You begin to relax and...*Wham! Wham! Wham!* "C'mon, have a heart. You have to get up! I *really* need this bread. My guest is really hungry. Please come help me out! I'm desperate!"

The nerve of some people. What unmitigated gall! Jesus closed His parable with these words:

> "I say to you, though he will not rise and give to him because he is his friend, yet because of his persistence he will rise and give him as many as he needs." (Luke 11:8)

It was not the neighbor's need, nor was it that neighborly friendship prevailed. It was desperation—importunity—that won the day. The brazen nerve of a neighbor who simply refused to take no for an answer. The bottom line? He created a tremendous ruckus and ruffled a lot of feathers...but he went home with loaves of bread tucked under each arm.

Jesus went on to make this point. He said, literally, *"Keep on asking* and you will receive. *Keep on seeking* and you will find. *Keep on knocking* and the door will be opened"* (see Matthew 7:7–8).

Let's be honest. Most of us don't approach God this way. We don't ask with tireless persistence. We don't seek with desperation. We don't want to make a nuisance of ourselves at the gates of heaven. We don't knock and knock and knock until the door finally opens. We don't wrestle with God all night long, as Jacob did. Neither do we echo Jacob's words and tell God through clenched teeth, "I will *not* let You go unless You bless me!" (Genesis 32:26).

It comes down to this:

How much do we truly hunger for God?

How much do we honestly desire personal revival?

How much do we truly want to turn back to the living God and walk in His ways?

How much do we long and thirst for our once-great nation to forsake her sin and unbelief, to turn back to God and His Word?

Enough to miss a meal or two as we fast and call on His name? Enough to lose some of our precious beauty sleep as we pray into the wee hours of the morning? Enough to bang on the doors of heaven until our hands ache and our knuckles bleed? Enough to create a ruckus? Enough to cry aloud in prayer until our throats are hoarse from pleading and our eyes are red from weeping?

If we want revival, we must humble ourselves and then pray in *desperation*, pray stretched-out prayers, as though our very lives depend on it.

And given the increasingly dangerous world in which we live, that may very well be the case.

Step Three

SEEK GOD'S FACE

You will seek Me and find Me,
when you search for Me with all your heart.
I will be found by you, says the LORD.

JEREMIAH 29:13–14

MOST OF US TEND TO THINK that praying and "seeking God's face" are one and the same.

But they are not.

Prayer often involves asking for something. We pray for wisdom, for health, for finances, for the salvation of loved ones, for our nation, and for a host of things too numerous to mention. Of course, we pray for revival, too, both in our own hearts and in our country.

But the ultimate—what the medieval theologians called the *summum bonum,* the greatest good—is to know God and draw near to Him.

This kind of prayer is not asking God to "do" something.

It is asking for His very presence.

It is pleading with Him to draw near to us and to linger.

We might imagine this intimacy with our awesome God to be unattainable. But if it were unattainable, why would He command it? David wrote:

When You said, "Seek My face,"
My heart said to You, "Your face, LORD, I will seek." (Psalm 27:8)

Seeking God's face is far different from asking Him for something or presenting Him with a list of petitions. For me, seeking the Lord's face means praying over and over and over again that I might be close to Him, be led by Him, have the knowledge of His will, and be used in His plan. It's amazing and wonderful how God answers this prayer. He makes me aware of His nearness at unexpected times.

On one occasion, for whatever reason, I was thinking about the incredible complexity of the human hormonal system. It's mind-boggling enough to realize that God created man in His image. But even more incredible to me is that He instilled in each human being a delicate mechanism that sends particular hormones throughout a person's body at each stage of development. This growth hormone progressively diminishes as people move toward the end of their lives. From this rather simple observation about human physiology grew an entirely new awareness of the immeasurable wisdom and majesty of our God, whose power spans the universe. I was lost in praise at the wonder and greatness of our God. He had indeed answered my prayer that I would sense His nearness to me.

Soon after that remarkable time of meditation, I began to think about the enormous responsibility that the Lord had taken on in creation. Then I thought about the grief and anguish He must experience as He sees people turning from Him, violating and even totally ignoring His commands, cursing Him, abusing one another, and living in poverty, disease, and hunger. None of this was His plan for the human beings He made in His image, the human beings His only Son died for on that cruel, rough-hewn cross.

"Why," I asked, *"did You even make us? And what kind of reward or benefit are You receiving from any aspect of Your creation?"*

His answer—the answer of my God, who came near in response to my prayers—was crystal clear: "I am creating a new heaven and a new earth. I am calling people from every nation, people who will love and serve Me. They will be with Me for all eternity. My call to you is to bring as many as you can to saving faith so that My new heaven and earth will be filled. Those in union with Jesus are My great reward out of all the creation." Once again I sensed with great joy the nearness of my God; the closeness of my heavenly Father.

Clearly, our God is a God of *relationship*. He is not a distant, hands-off God. He numbers the very hairs on our heads. He knows the words on our tongues before we speak them. He ordained the days of our lives even before we took our first breath.

He doesn't want us to be like little children, full of

immature requests for things from their parents. Instead, He wants us to go to Him as mature sons or daughters who know their Father, who are in tune with His will, who have begun to think and act like the Father, and who can responsibly serve in the Father's kingdom. God wants us to move beyond the petition stage of prayer to a time when the ultimate good—in fact the only good—is being in communion with Him.

We are told in Genesis that, after creation, God walked in the Garden of Eden in the cool of the evening. There He communed with the humans He had made in His image. He talked to them and they to Him. They saw Him because there was no sin to obscure their vision of Him.

To "seek God's face," then, is to strive to restore that intimate bond of fellowship between God and man that goes back to creation.

The opening chapter of John's Gospel tells us that "In the beginning was the Word, and the Word was with God, and the Word was God" (v. 1). The Greek word translated *with* is *pros*, which means more precisely "face-to-face." So we might write it, "In the beginning the Word [Jesus] was face-to-face with the Father."

Is this not the relationship we should earnestly seek as we pray for revival?

Let me ask you another question. Have you ever had the experience of sensing the Lord's presence so keenly that you were afraid to move or breathe for fear that He might withdraw that nearness? I like reading the biblical accounts of men and women who invited God to come to them and linger with them. To stay just a little bit longer.

In almost every case, that's exactly what He does.

"DON'T PASS ON BY!"

In Genesis 18, Abraham looked up from the doorway of his tent one hot afternoon to see three men standing in front of him in the shade of some large oak trees. How had they approached so silently? Although Scripture doesn't say for sure, I believe that Abraham must have known right away who had come calling that day. These weren't three ordinary, travel-weary tourists hiking across Canaan. This was the Lord Himself, in human form, accompanied by two mighty angels.

There was no way Abraham was going to let these visitors pass on by! If indeed this was a divine visitation, he was going to make the most of it.

> When he saw them, he ran from the tent door
> to meet them, and bowed himself to the
> ground, and said, "My Lord, if I have now
> found favor in Your sight, *do not pass on by
> Your servant.* Please let a little water be
> brought, and wash your feet, and rest your-
> selves under the tree. And I will bring a morsel
> of bread, that you may refresh your hearts.
> After that you may pass by, inasmuch as you
> have come to your servant." (Genesis 18:2–5)

"Do not pass on by Your servant!" Have you ever
prayed a prayer like that?[1] Have you ever asked the
Lord to come to you, surround you with His presence,
and stay with you through the long hours of the day or
the dark watches of the night?

One stormy night, out on the Sea of Galilee, Jesus
went to His disciples, walking on the water through
the storm.

> About the fourth watch of the night He came
> to them, walking on the sea, and would have

passed them by. And when they saw Him walking on the sea, they supposed it was a ghost, and cried out; for they all saw Him and were troubled. But immediately He talked with them and said to them, "Be of good cheer! It is I; do not be afraid." Then He went up into the boat to them, and the wind ceased. (Mark 6:48–51)

Mark tells us that He "would have passed them by." But they cried out in their fear, and He went to them to comfort them and encourage their hearts. Before long, He had climbed into the boat with them, and the storm was just a memory, like a bad dream.

If the Lord is in the neighborhood, if you sense His nearness, don't let Him pass on by! Invite Him to linger. Is there room for Him in your boat? *Make room*—even if you have to pitch some things overboard. Ask Him to stay in your boat always. Don't try to weather the storm alone.

One of my favorite stories in the New Testament takes place after our Lord has risen from the dead. Remember when He encountered Cleopas and his friend on the road to Emmaus? The two men trudged wearily home from Jerusalem that dismal Sunday afternoon, their hearts and hopes shattered by the crucifixion and death of the One they had known as Teacher, Master, and Lord. Suddenly the risen Christ walked alongside them, but they didn't recognize Him.

What a walk that turned out to be! Jesus took them book by book through the Old Testament, from Genesis through all the prophets, and showed them how the Messiah had to suffer disgrace and death before He entered in to His glory. Later, they would reflect, "Did not our heart burn within us while He talked with us on the road, and while He opened the Scriptures to us?" (Luke 24:32).

When they finally arrived at the house in Emmaus, some seven miles from Jerusalem, Jesus was saying goodbye and heading on down the road. Luke says, "He acted as though He were going farther" (v. 28, NASB).

But the two men would have none of it. They were captivated by this mysterious Traveler, who somehow seemed so very familiar.

> They urged him strongly, saying, "Stay with us, for it is toward evening and the day is now far spent." So he went in to stay with them. When

he was at table with them, he took the bread
and blessed and broke it and gave it to them.
And their eyes were opened. (vv. 29–31, ESV).

"Stay with us!" They didn't let Jesus walk on by.
These two men strongly urged Him to stay and dine
with them. And as they prepared to share that meal,
the Lord blessed it and suddenly opened their eyes to
what they had not seen before. Surprise and uncon-
tainable joy swept through the room like a gust of
wind through an open window.

The Lord Jesus will dine with you, too, when you
plead with Him not to walk on by, when you strongly
urge Him to stay. It's not as though you have to overcome
His unwillingness. In fact, He stands at the door of your
life and knocks, just waiting for a dinner invitation.

"See, I stand knocking at the door. If anyone
listens to my voice and opens the door, I will
go into his house and dine with him, and he
with me." (Revelation 3:20, Phillips)

Accept this invitation by seeking God's face, by
asking Him to teach you to be in communion with

Him moment by moment throughout your day, and by not letting Him pass on by when you sense Him near you.

Step Four

TURN FROM SIN

Plow the hard ground of your hearts,
for now is the time to seek the Lord.

HOSEA 10:12, TLB

OUR CBN PRAYER COUNSELORS receive eight to ten
thousand calls every weekday.

The mail department sends out twenty to thirty
million pieces of mail each year.

We distribute six million pounds of food to the
poor in America every month.

Our television programs reach tens of millions of people around the world with the good news of Jesus Christ each month, and millions have come to recognize Him as their Savior and Lord.

Our worldwide ministry is exciting and demanding, and that kind of intensity can take its toll.

In the midst of all this activity—which, ironically, is designed to save the lost and strengthen believers—we can and do become more professional than relational. Somewhere among the schedules, the deadlines, and the paperwork, we lose some of our passion to win the lost. Although our purpose is to serve the Lord and although we care deeply about people's great need for Jesus, nevertheless in our busyness we lose some of our compelling love for Him and for people who don't yet know Him. The sweet anointing of the Lord's power begins to fade from us and from our efforts as we become more mechanical than heartfelt and God-directed.

At some point, by God's grace, we suddenly realize that we are merely going through the motions of service and ministry. We acknowledge that a layer of crust has begun to form on the soil of our hearts. We recognize that we need to break up that fallow ground—and we are hardly the first believers to need to experience this change of heart. Listen to what the prophet Hosea wrote:

> Sow for yourselves righteousness;
> Reap in mercy;
> Break up your fallow ground,
> For it is time to seek the LORD,
> Till He comes and rains righteousness on you.
>   (Hosea 10:12)

What does it mean to break up your fallow, or unplowed, ground? We at CBN are very intentional about breaking up the crust that can all too easily begin to form in our lives. In fact, we even try to prevent such hardening! We have two special weeks of prayer, two holidays for fasting and prayer, prayer meetings every working day, and an all-staff prayer time once a week.

To break up the fallow ground of my own heart, I personally take several days between Christmas and New Year's Day to pray and to seek God for direction, and six days every week throughout the year I spend early morning time in personal devotions.

Why are such devotional times so critical to spiritual growth? Why can't we let our fallow heart lie still for a while? If you've lived all your life in the city, let me offer an explanation of a basic farming principle: If a field is left idle without planting or cultivation, it will develop a hard crust. The combined action of the rain, the sun, and the wind over a period of months—or sometimes even years—makes the hard ground progressively harder.

You might come along and sow seed on that ground, but it would be like throwing seed on an asphalt parking lot. The birds would love it, but seed doesn't germinate in asphalt! It simply won't penetrate. And just like in that asphalt parking lot, the moisture won't soak in to fallow ground. It will either puddle up or roll off into gullies and streams.

How do you work with ground like that? How do you return it to productive service once again so that it receives the good seed and the life-giving moisture?

It won't be easy. It's going to take a sharp plow.

In order to bring such a field into cultivation, a massive turning plow must be run through it, followed by crisscross disking to break the clods into fine earth suitable to receive seed and moisture.

The spiritual life of believers tends to be like that. If we neglect the cultivation of our heart, the soil begins to harden. It's inevitable! Our hearts can also become hardened because we are preoccupied with the things of this world. It might even be because we are busy with good and godly things rather than the best things, those things that God has specifically called us to during this particular season of life.

Whatever the reasons for the hardening of our hearts, the process may look something like this: First, we begin to skip our Bible reading and prayer time. This is nearly always the first step away from the Lord. We plan on getting back into it, but days go by, and we just don't. After all, we're *so busy*—and the Lord understands, doesn't He? Then we begin to miss some of the meetings with other believers that we used to regularly attend and even look forward to. We drop out of the weekly Bible study or the men's prayer breakfast. We don't return the calls of Christian friends. We find it easier and easier to skip attendance at Sunday worship. (After all, we can worship God out in nature, can't we?)

Old sin habits begin to return. Thoughts and

actions that once caused our spirit pain and remorse now begin to take root again. Instead of desiring the approval of God and fellowship with Jesus, we find ourselves caught up in the desire for money, things, more and bigger possessions. As time goes on, we fill our mind with pictures, sounds, and concepts that are light years away from a walk with Christ. Our language becomes coarser. We associate more and more with those who rebel against God…and we begin to agree with them.

We can hear preaching or Christian music, but it doesn't move us as it once did. We may even find ourselves starting to behave in ways that we clearly know are wrong, but our conscience—which for so long gave us clear warnings that we were straying from God's safe and narrow path—doesn't seem to work anymore.

Our hearts are hardened, and that crust must be broken. But how do we begin?

A PLAN FOR REPENTANCE

The way is simple. We don't sin in generalities, so we should not repent in generalities. The prayer "O God,

pardon my sins and transgressions, for they are many"
won't cut it.

Allow me to suggest a plan. Get alone in a quiet
place and take a writing pad and pen with you. Get on
your knees and tell God that you have come to Him to
repent of your sins and ask His forgiveness. Admit to
Him that the soil of your soul has become hard and
that you need His help to "break up the fallow
ground."

Plan on setting aside adequate time for this. Don't
be in a hurry. This process may take hours—even
days—and may require repeating.

In your time of prayer, echo the words of the
psalmist:

> Create in me a clean heart, O God,
> And renew a steadfast spirit within me.
>   (51:10)

> Let the words of my mouth and the medita-
>   tion of my heart
> Be acceptable in Your sight,
> O LORD, my strength and my Redeemer.
>   (19:14)

Search me, O God, and know my heart:
try me, and know my thoughts:
And see if there be any wicked way in me,
and lead me in the way everlasting.
  (139:23–24, KJV)

Allow the Holy Spirit to begin the process of bringing to mind what you should write. Be brutal on yourself! Don't excuse anything that is even vaguely wrong. The object is to confess, forsake, find mercy and forgiveness—and then, forgiven and cleansed, enter the presence of the Lord.

I repeat, don't hurry! The process isn't fast, nor is it painless. But—approached sincerely and honestly—it is always worthwhile.

Years ago when I was in seminary, I remember following these steps. I knelt before the Lord with an open notebook and began to make a list of my sins. Nothing was particularly surprising to me right away. But just a few days later, God opened my eyes to a truth about myself that had the potential to destroy me.

God showed me that though I had brought my life in surrender to the Cross, I had never surrendered my financial ambitions. Many of the long-range, self-centered goals I had carried over from my business days still had a grip on my heart. I needed not only to confess these selfish goals, but also to allow the Holy Spirit to burn them out of my inner man.

The following process helped that whole painful, wonderful process to take place in my heart. With all my heart, I encourage you to walk that path yourself. In God's wonderful grace, many will follow you. (See Psalm 40:3.)

Begin with the great commandment . . .

"You shall love the LORD your God with all your heart, with all your soul, and with all your mind" (Matthew 22:37). We've all broken this one, so write it down.

Confess the deadness and coldness of your devotional life.

You no longer pray as you once did. You have neglected the study of the Bible. You have lost your first love. Write these things down in the simplest of terms.

Reconcile with those who have hurt or offended you.

Jesus said, "If you bring your gift to the altar, and there remember that your brother has something against you, leave your gift there before the altar, and go your way. First be reconciled to your brother, and then come and offer your gift" (Matthew 5:23–24). Think now of the people who have really mistreated you or slandered you. These are people you may have resented for years, perhaps even hated. Write their names down, forgive them, and ask forgiveness for hating them.

Admit your dishonesty.

The Holy Spirit is the Spirit of truth. Have you allowed any misrepresentations or outright lies to remain outstanding with your acquaintances and friends? Any exaggerations on your résumé? This acknowledgment can be painful, but write down the times you've been less than honest. Write down *all* of them. You may have some fixing to do on these, but you will find that honesty brings genuine relief.

Clean up areas of sexual impurity.

Chances are better than average that you've been struggling with some form of impurity or sexual sin. There is an overpowering amount of sexual solicitation in our world, and it is aimed at the carnal nature of adults and teens alike. Your heavenly Father understands the temptation, but He still wants you to lay your sins and failures before Him.

Write down the temptations, the transgressions, the problems—privately. Keep them between you and God. Then tell Satan that this is all covered by the sacrifice of Jesus Christ and that he, as your enemy and deceiver, has wasted his effort to destroy you.

Repent of any slander.

Slander is a terrible sin, but one that we all take lightly. Write down whom you have slandered and when. Again, do not give yourself the benefit of the doubt. Your heavenly Father knows it all, and He waits for you to come to Him openly and honestly so that He can forgive you.

Admit that you have grieved or quenched God's Spirit.

Let the Holy Spirit reveal to you the times when your words have grieved Him, the times when you have disobeyed Him, the times when you have wounded others, the times when you have been insensitive to the spiritual or physical need of someone you could have helped. Think of the resentment that you have caused in others by your conduct. Think of people whom you have cheated or abused. Think of what you may have taken that is not yours. Think of the times when your life and actions have actually damaged someone else's faith.

Write down all these things. Take your time. Not only will this exercise bring God's power into your life, but it will also serve as a welcome catharsis to your mind and spirit.

Get things right with your family.

The Bible tells men to make peace with their wives lest their prayers be hindered. There is no way that you can enter into God's presence while harboring anger, resentment, bitterness, jealousy, or unforgivingness against your spouse.

Write down the problems you have caused your mate and the hurts and offenses he or she has experienced because of your words, your actions, and your attitudes. Remember that this is not a blame game. The purpose of this time with the Lord is for you to honestly confess your sin and guilt. You must be honest with yourself and about yourself. Do not try to justify your actions. God knows what is right and what is wrong.

The Bible says,

> The sacrifices of God are a broken spirit,
> A broken and a contrite heart—
> These, O God, You will not despise. (Psalm 51:17)

> God resists the proud,
> But gives grace to the humble. (1 Peter 5:5)

As you remember and write down the ways that you have wronged your mate, think also of the ways you have wronged your children. Have you consistently loved them with a love that points them to their heavenly Father? Have you brought them up in the knowledge and admonition of the Lord? Have you been so rigid and authoritarian that they have rebelled against you as well as against the Lord? Have you been available to talk, to listen carefully to them, and to understand their problems, hopes, and dreams?

Think, too, of your attitude toward your own parents. If you are currently living with your mother and father, are you showing them the honor and respect God calls you to? If you have elderly parents, have you loved them, cared for them, and paid them the attention they deserve?

When you finish praying through this time of confession, you may have written down quite a long list of sins—things you've done that God did not want you to do and things God wanted you to do that you didn't do. Go through your list once more. At each point, earnestly ask God's forgiveness. Where an ongoing wrong continues, promise yourself and the Lord that you will make it right—and ask for His help. Pray not only that His Holy Spirit will convict you when you sin, but also—and better yet—that He will keep you from sinning.

Then take your list and say, "Lord, all these sins and transgressions I place under the blood of Jesus

Christ. I accept Your gracious forgiveness, and I praise You for setting me free. I humbly ask that I may walk in Your presence, that You may hear my prayer, and that You will send revival to heal my land. In Jesus' name, amen."

Then take a match and burn your list before the Lord, remembering these words from Scripture:

> For as the heavens are high above the earth,
> So great is His mercy toward those who fear
>   Him;
> As far as the east is from the west,
> So far has He removed our transgressions
>   from us.
> As a father pities his children,
> So the LORD pities those who fear Him.
> For He knows our frame;
> He remembers that we are dust.
>   (Psalm 103:11–14)

Spend time worshiping and adoring God for who He is and what He has done for you. God has forgiven you! The price for your sin has been paid once and for all by Jesus Christ. You are free! You are cleansed! The

Bible tells us that we have been washed clean from a guilty conscience to serve the living God. God does not want you to be engaged in morbid introspection all your life long. He wants you to enter joyously into His service as a full-fledged member of His holy family.

If Satan seeks to accuse you or discourage you or attack you with something on your list that you have already confessed, forsaken, and burned into ashes, refuse to allow it! Open your Bible, and oppose him with the words of 1 John 1:9:

> If we confess our sins, He is faithful and just
> to forgive us our sins and to cleanse us from all
> unrighteousness.

As we live our lives in God's presence, we can experience an ongoing cleansing from sin. The apostle John said it this way: "But if we walk in the light as He is in the light, we have fellowship with one another, and the blood of Jesus Christ His Son cleanses us from all sin" (1 John 1:7).

Now that your conscience has been made tender before the Lord, you will naturally walk with Him in His light. But keep short accounts with God. If you sin, confess it immediately and *put it behind you.*

You are prepared for *life again,* right now. But could a revival among His people begin with *you?* It can.

Step Five

PRAY WITH FELLOW BELIEVERS

"Again I say to you that if two of you agree on earth concerning anything that they ask, it will be done for them by My Father in heaven. For where two or three are gathered together in My name, I am there in the midst of them."

MATTHEW 18:19–20

ON THE DAY OF PENTECOST, the disciples were together in one place, and their hearts were in one accord.

We should not be surprised, then, that the Bible warns us, "Let us not give up meeting together, as some are in the habit of doing, but let us encourage one another—and all the more as you see the Day approaching" (Hebrews 10:25, NIV).

Each of us needs to find a private place of quiet to do the kind of deep soul-searching I have described, but the Bible also calls us to join with fellow believers for prayer. In fact, every classic revival of which I am aware took place when believers had gathered together, their hearts in one accord, in one place—whether that place was a church, a tabernacle, a barn, or a clearing in the woods.

Obviously, the leaders of such revivals need to spend large amounts of time alone in earnest prayer and study.

- Evan Roberts, the leader of the Welsh revival, had a glorious encounter with the fire of the living God at one o'clock in the morning as he was praying in his bedroom.
- Charles Finney, America's foremost advocate of revival, met the Holy Spirit while he was praying in his study. He reported the glorious

experience as if "giant wings fanned his face." Then he was lifted into a new experience of the presence of God.

- John Hyde of India prayed alone for six to eight hours a day.
- It was said that James, the Lord's brother, had knees like a camel because of the hours that he spent alone on his knees in prayer.

Each of us can and must spend time alone with the Lord, but the visitation from God we are seeking may very well come only when believers are praying together. And I assure you that there is nothing quite like that kind of visitation! But I'll get to that in a minute.

First, realize that when you gather with fellow believers to pray together and seek God's face "in one accord," you'll find it wonderful for your own soul.

On April 29, 1980, I was privileged to be the program co-chairman for a unique assembly called "Washington for Jesus." Some five hundred thousand people gathered that day on the Mall in Washington, D.C., between the Washington Monument and the United States Capitol building. Not surprisingly, that half a million was an eclectic group.

They came from different backgrounds and different stations in life.

Some were young; some were old.

Some were educated; some were not.

Some were poor; some were well-to-do.

They were Asians, Hispanics, and blacks.

There were men, women, teenagers, and little ones.

They were from dozens of denominations, or no denomination at all.

Yet all day this diverse group of believers stood together, sat together, sang together, and prayed together. They listened to messages from God's Word and sought His face "in one accord." All were there to pray for America and to believe God that Jesus Christ would be Lord of Washington and America.

Without question, their prayers—prayed in community and with hearts "in one accord"—were answered. There was a change of administration in Washington. Hope replaced malaise. Policies were put in place that resulted in the fall of communism in the Soviet Union. The foundation was laid for two decades of unprecedented prosperity. The war that many feared did not happen. In the next five years, millions of people were added to the church.

Once again, our ever-faithful God answered the fervent prayers of those who prayed "in one accord." But don't assume for even a second that He responds only to the prayers of a large gathering. In fact, praying in one accord may involve a very small gathering—perhaps just two or three people. To begin, there may be a small core of those whose hearts are knit together in their desire for personal holiness and their hunger for a visitation of God. It would be unwise to expect everyone who professes to be a Christian to share that kind of zeal. That will come later.

The goal is a group, small or large, gathered together "in one accord"—with one heart and one desire. Petty differences among participants must be put aside along with disputes over fine points of doctrine. Whether someone's eschatology makes him premillennial, postmillennial, or amillennial is of absolutely no consequence if that individual is crying out for a fresh touch from God.

As prayer for revival begins, the time is right to ask forgiveness of those you have offended as well as to openly forgive those who have offended you. Put aside the petty spite and jealousy that may have character-ized your relationships with other members of your church family. God is love. As you seek Him, let His love work through you to tear down all the barriers that keep you from loving your brothers and sisters in Christ.

When the power of God descends, all those things that look like reasons for us to be separated from each other fade into insignificance in the light of God's glory. Remember also God's solemn assessment of the human unity He observed at the tower of Babel.

> The LORD came down to see the city and the tower which the sons of men had built. The LORD said, "Behold, they are one people, and they all have the same language. And this is what they began to do, and now nothing which they purpose to do will be impossible for them." (Genesis 11:5–6, NASB)

Just think of the incredible power of human endeavor when those involved were united—even in rebellion against God. Then think of the awesome power that our unity can produce when we are energized by the power of the Holy Spirit in revival. This is the power to change a nation and to frustrate the plans of those who wish to destroy us.

Is it any wonder that Satan—who knows full well what a church praying "in one accord" and empowered by the Holy Spirit can accomplish—does everything in his power to cause rancor and division among Christians and to entice them to sin so that the power of the Holy Spirit in their lives will be lessened? Satan trembles at the mere thought of revival among God's people.

Attacks on America and attacks on God's people in America will come and go. But out of the tragedy caused by hate, the church of Jesus Christ will arise as the mighty spiritual force that God intended, and, in the words of our Lord, *"the gates of hell shall not prevail against it."*

Step Six

PERSEVERE

*For you have need of endurance,
so that after you have done the will of God,
you may receive the promise.*

Hebrews 10:36

JUST BEFORE THE RISEN CHRIST ascended into heaven,
He left some very specific instructions for His small
band of followers.

The command was perfectly clear.

But it wasn't what they wanted to hear.

Jesus said, *"Wait."* And then He left the planet.

And being assembled together with them, He commanded them not to depart from Jerusalem, but to *wait* for the Promise of the Father, "which," He said, "you have heard from Me; for John truly baptized with water, but you shall be baptized with the Holy Spirit not many days from now." (Acts 1:4–5)

So it was that 120 men and women went into Jerusalem, found sanctuary in a large second-story room, and began to pray and wait for the promise of the Father.

Jesus had promised that they would receive something. Someone. Sometime. But He didn't say precisely how, and He didn't say precisely when. "Not many days from now"? In their minds, that probably meant two or three.

Day one passed without event. There was no change; there was no miracle.

Then day two—nothing.

Day three. Still nothing.

Then came days four, five, six, seven, eight, and

nine. The upstairs room began to feel smaller. Cramped. *Not many days from now? What did You mean, Lord? Couldn't You have been just a little more specific?* Imagine their impatience. Imagine their fear. Imagine their struggle to hold on to their faith. Imagine the restless boredom of sitting in one place day after day with nothing happening.

Was their hope merely an illusion? Jesus was not there in person. Had He deceived them? Was their prayer vigil merely a vain hope? Something symbolic, but without substance? Other doubts may have assailed them, but they went on waiting and they went on praying, just as they had been instructed to do. They held on to the promise of their Lord even when nothing made sense. They held His words tightly to their hearts, and they persevered.

Persevere is one of the great words of the New Testament and the Christian faith.

In our English Bibles, the Greek word *hupomone* is translated *perseverance, patience,* or *endurance.* It's a rich, multilayered term that speaks of steadfastness, constancy, and cheerful patience. It describes those who abide under difficult situations and who do so with courage and hope.

You won't win many friends or be elected to a public office in America today by counseling patience and perseverance. It's not a popular term in our culture and hasn't been for years. We don't want to wait; we don't want to have to persevere. Just a few days ago, for example, I came across an electronics catalog with this slogan right in the middle of the cover: "Experience INSTANT gratification!" The article went on to describe a digital camera with such immediate results that you can "share memories as fast as they happen."

Evidence all around supports the well-established fact that we Americans don't like to wait. We have created a civilization in which everything is geared toward quick resolution and rapid gratification. We want to eat fast, learn fast, travel fast, communicate fast, dine fast, and shop fast. We want swift service on our insurance claims, rocket speed on our computer processors, and rapid advancement and pay increases in our jobs.

Nor do we think that persevering through suffering is a valid concept. We demand immediate results for our health problems, rapid and complete pain relief, and if our mate or our marriage isn't what we had hoped for or imagined…well, get out as fast as you can and go look for something better.

But the Bible has a different idea. God's Word tells us that it is good to wait, good to endure, good to hold on to our faith through long days and stormy nights. "For you have need of endurance," the writer of Hebrews tells his readers, "so that after you have done the will of God, you may receive the promise."

The true Christian life is all about believing, obeying, waiting, and enduring. But it isn't some grim, grit-your-teeth, tighten-your-belt brand of stoicism. In fact, biblical persevering is almost always tied to hope.

Paul wanted with all his heart to get that message across to the Roman believers. He'd never met these men and women, so he didn't have a single face in mind as he wrote to them. But God had given him a deep love for these brothers and sisters who lived at the throbbing center of the civilized world. Paul longed to see them. He ached to impart the knowledge and wisdom that would help them live for Jesus even in the midst of suffering and persecution. He wrote:

> And not only that, but we also glory in tribulations, knowing that tribulation produces perseverance; and perseverance, character; and character, hope. Now hope does not disappoint,

because the love of God has been poured out in our hearts by the Holy Spirit who was given to us. (Romans 5:3–5)

Don't despise the hard times, Paul was saying.

Don't think the world has ended or that your Lord has forgotten you or somehow misplaced your file. In God's ledger books—the only ones that truly count— tribulations and troubles are never a waste of time. As you endure them with patience, your inner character begins to take on muscle fiber and definition.

And then something unexpected and wonderful begins to happen to you.

You begin to experience hope where you never thought to find it. It begins like the simplest melody, almost inaudible, riding on a distant wind. Gradually, inexorably, it swells into a mighty symphony.

This hope—true, durable, biblical hope—is perhaps the best thing you can know in this life. It sustains the soul like meat and bread, and it gladdens the heart like wine. It endures despite everything this world can throw at you; it shines in the deepest darkness; it outlasts diamonds.

But this hope doesn't come cheap. Biblical hope

roots itself in dark days and desolate places, sends out its branches in the storm, and flowers in hours of crushing pressure and anxiety. The world has no idea what it is or where it came from or how it survives. But those of God's children who have experienced it know that it is eminently worth waiting for.

> But if we hope for what we do not see, we eagerly wait for it with perseverance. (Romans 8:25)

> Indeed we count them blessed who endure. You have heard of the perseverance of Job and seen the end intended by the Lord—that the Lord is very compassionate and merciful. (James 5:11)

That little band of disciples in the upper room endured the long waiting, and they held on to their hope. Then, when the Day of Pentecost, the fiftieth day after the Passover, finally came, the miracle happened. The Bible tells us that a sound like a mighty rushing wind filled the room where they were sitting, and cloven tongues of fire separated and appeared over the heads of every person there. Then each person in the room was filled with the Holy Spirit and began to speak other languages as the Spirit gave them utterance.

The noise was so loud that a crowd gathered, made up of people from all over the Roman Empire. They listened in amazement to these simple, uneducated Galileans speaking in each of their native languages.

Some made fun of the believers, but most people in the crowd were so overwhelmed by God's power that they listened eagerly to Peter as he preached to them. Then they cried out, "What should we do?" That day, Peter, who only a few weeks before had been afraid of a servant girl, preached with such authority and power that three thousand were converted to faith in the Lord Jesus Christ.

Do you realize that the same God who visited His people at Pentecost in Jerusalem wants to visit His church today?

It's time to press in, my friend. Follow the steps to revival set forth in the pages of this little book....

Humble yourself. Let the brightness and beauty of His holy presence reveal how dependent you are upon His forgiveness and grace.

Pray with every fiber of your being. Call on the Lord with a desperate intensity, refusing to be distracted by the cares and toys of our shallow culture.

Seek God's face above all else. If you sense His nearness, don't let Him pass on by. Cry out for His presence as if crying out for water in an arid wilderness.

Turn from all known sin. Allow God's Spirit the time and opportunity to search the very depths of your heart.

Pray with fellow believers regularly, with your hearts "in one accord" regarding the issues of faith that matter most. Discover the energy, joy, and power of joining your prayer to that of two or three others—or maybe thousands!

And finally, *persevere in all these things.* Hold on to faith, patience, and steadfast hope in the face of all that Satan or a godless world might throw at you.

Do what you can to turn your eyes upon Jesus. Then wait for God to do what only He can do.

Revival in your own heart can begin today. Revival in the nation we love can also begin today. After all, when revival happens, it will happen one heart at a time.

Notes

1. My friend Dr. Jack Hayford cited this event in his wonderful book *Pursuing the Will of God* (Sisters, Ore.: Multnomah Publishers, 1997).

The publisher and author would love to hear your comments about this book. *Please contact us at:*
www.lifechangebooks.com

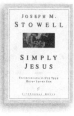